P9-DNT-692

Alfred's

Music for Little Mozarts

Coloring and Ear Training Activities to Bring Out the Music in Every Young Child

Cover illustration and interior art by Christine Finn

Christine H. Barden · Gayle Kowalchyk · E. L. Lancaster

ISBN 0-7390-0651-7

Foreword

Recent studies suggest that playing and listening to music at a young age improves learning, memory, reasoning ability and general creativity. Research also supports the theory that young children who are exposed to music develop enhanced cognitive skills. The *Music for Little Mozarts* series was written to provide appropriate piano instruction for four-, five- and six-year-olds while simultaneously developing listening skills. The series was designed to provide a balance between the discipline necessary for playing the instrument and the enjoyment one gets from the process of music-making.

The course centers around the adventures of Beethoven Bear and Mozart Mouse as they learn about music. Three books at each level guide the children through a comprehensive approach to musical learning. In the *Music Lesson Book*, students are introduced to new musical concepts and performance of pieces at the piano as they follow the story of Beethoven Bear and Mozart Mouse. Plush animals of the two characters are integral to making the course fun for young students. The *Music Workbook* contains carefully designed pages to color, that reinforce the musical concepts introduced in the Music Lesson Book. In addition, well-planned listening activities develop ear-training skills. The *Music Discovery Book* contains songs that allow the students to experience music through singing, movement and response to rhythm patterns. Music appreciation is fostered through carefully chosen music that introduces the students to great music through the ages. Melodies to sing, using either solfege or letter names, help students learn to match pitch and discover tonal elements of music. Correlated compact disc recordings for materials in the Music Lesson and Music Discovery Books are essential to achieve the goals of the course. General MIDI disks also are available for students or teachers who have the necessary equipment. A Starter Kit includes a music bag for carrying lesson materials, a music activity board and the two plush animal characters (Beethoven Bear and Mozart Mouse). Plush animals for Nannerl Mouse and Haydn Hippo are available separately.

Role of Parents: The teacher serves as a musical guide for young students in fostering their curiosity, natural ability and interest, but parents also play an important role in guiding their child's musical training. The authors recommend that parents attend lessons with their child and participate actively in the learning process. Parents will need to read the directions to their child during daily practice. Regularity of practice is important; short practice sessions of 10–15 minutes are suggested for young students, with activities changing frequently within the practice time. (Teachers can give valuable suggestions regarding practice.) Patience, sincere praise and a show of enthusiasm about new materials will be very beneficial. A musical partnership between parents and child in a nurturing environment provides quality time for fostering important family relationships.

Notes to the Teacher: The course is easy to use both in private and group lessons. Through careful pacing and reinforcement, appealing music with clever lyrics is introduced in the Music Lesson Book. The Music Workbook and Music Discovery Books are correlated page by page with the Music Lesson Book to provide well-balanced lessons. A separate *Teacher's Handbook* offers suggestions and lesson plans to aid the teacher with planning. All books contain clean and uncluttered pages, clear music engraving and attractive artwork to complement the music and appeal to young children.

About the Music Workbook, Book 4: The Music Workbook reinforces each concept presented in the Music Lesson Book through carefully designed pages for children to color. It also specifically focuses on the training and development of the ear. (Suggested listening examples for ear training pages are given in the Teacher's Handbook.) This book is coordinated page by page with the Music Lesson Book and assignments are ideally made according to the instructions in the upper right corner of each page of the Music Workbook. Many students enjoy completing these pages so much that they will want to work beyond the assigned material. However, it is best to wait until the indicated pages in the Music Lesson Book have been covered before the corresponding material in this book is studied.

The authors and publisher of this course offer our best wishes to children, parents and teachers as you begin this new adventure. It is certain to be richly rewarding!

Table of Contents

4

Use with Alfred's *Music for Little Mozarts*,
Lesson Book 4, page 4.

C Position Review

1. Color the areas containing a C **yellow**.
2. Color the areas containing a D **purple**.
3. Color the areas containing an E **pink**.
4. Color the areas containing an F **blue**.
5. Color the areas containing a G **green**.

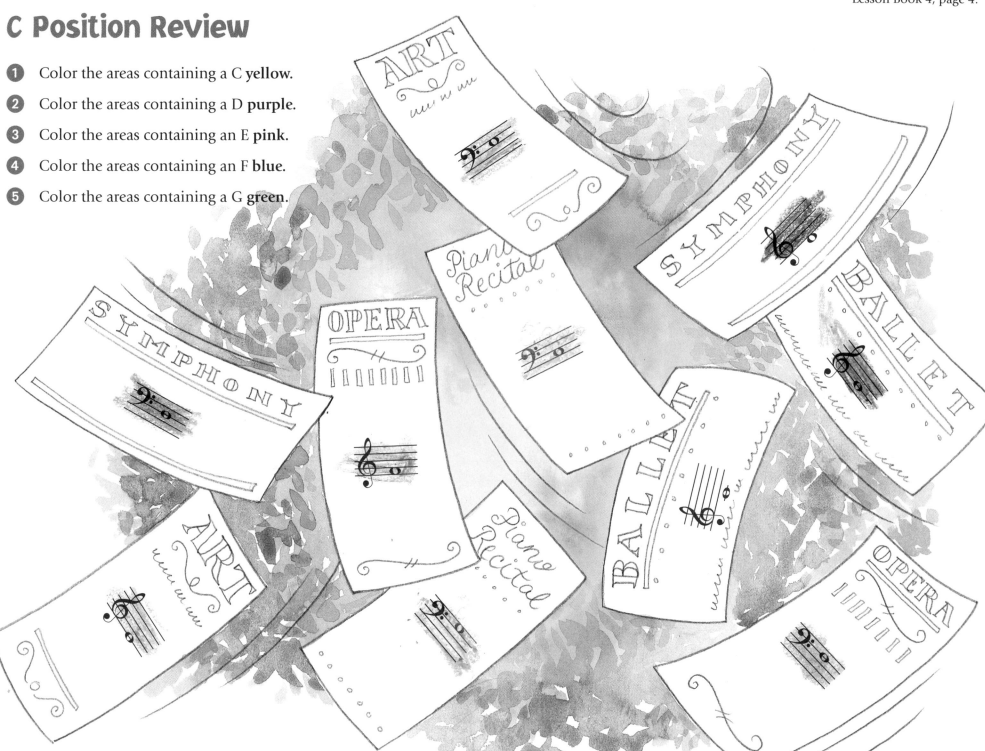

Melodic Intervals

Identify each interval, then play it on the keyboard.

- Circle 2 for the 2nd.
- Circle 3 for the 3rd.
- Circle 4 for the 4th.
- Circle 5 for the 5th.

1

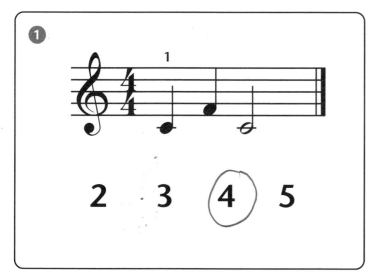

2   3   (4)   5

2

(2)   3   4   5

3

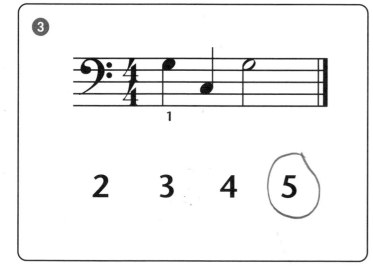

2   3   4   (5)

4

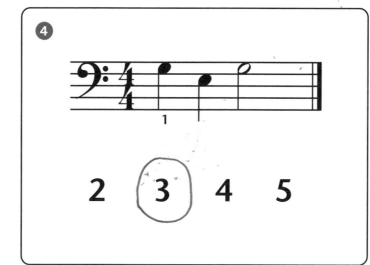

2   (3)   4   5

Melodic and Harmonic Intervals

1 Using a **blue** crayon, circle the notes that are played separately (melodic intervals).

2 Using a **red** crayon, circle the notes that are played together (harmonic intervals).

Rhythm Patterns in ¾ and 4/4 Time

Your teacher will clap a rhythm pattern.

● Circle the pattern that you hear.

★

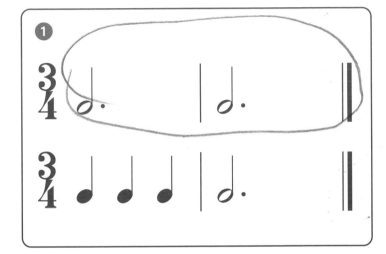

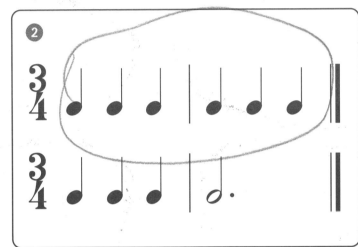

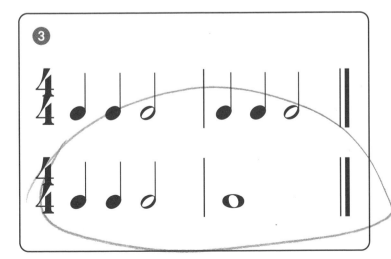

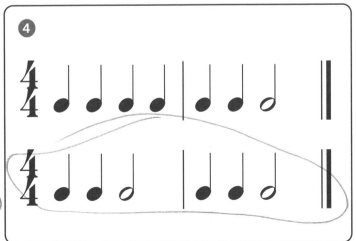

Hands Together

Use with page 8.

Using a **yellow** crayon, circle the examples that are played hands together.

Same and Different

Circle J. S. Bunny if the harmonic intervals are the same.

Circle Nina Ballerina if the harmonic intervals are different.

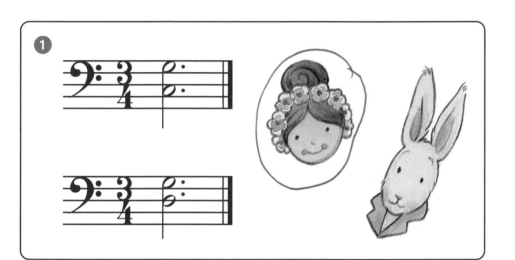

Middle C Position Review

1. Color the areas containing an A **green**.
2. Color the areas containing a B **brown**.
3. Color the areas containing a C **pink**.
4. Color the areas containing a D **orange**.
5. Color the areas containing an E **red**.
6. Color the areas containing an F **blue**.
7. Color the areas containing a G **gray**.

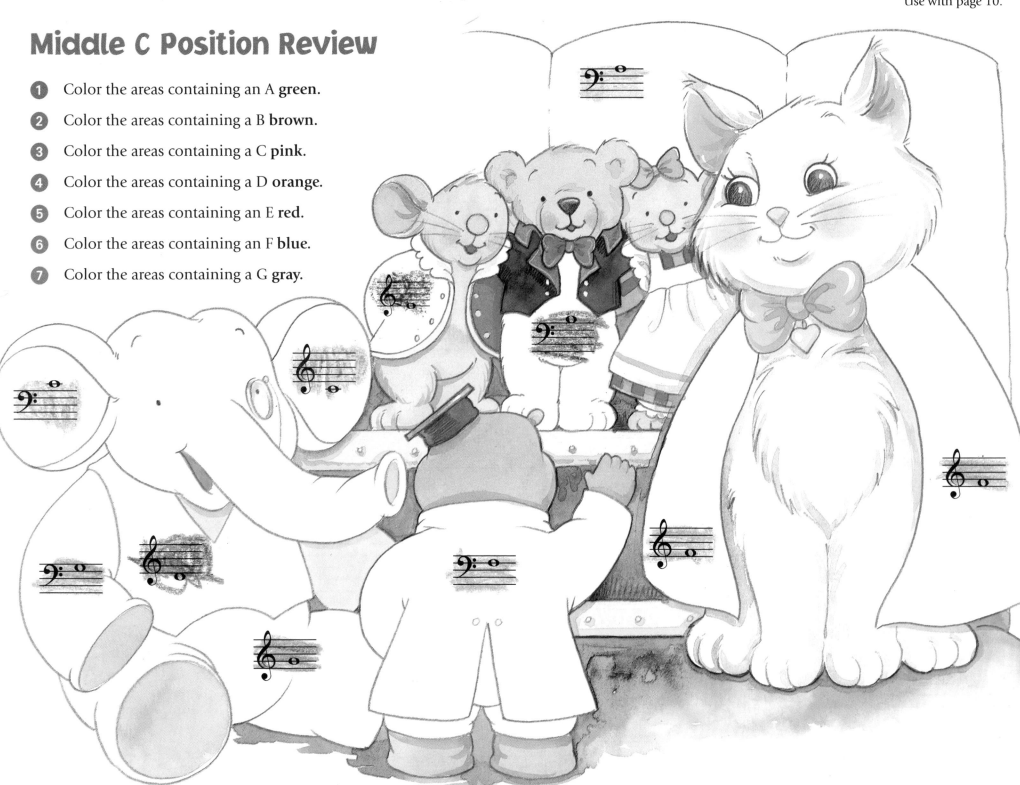

2nds, 3rds and 4ths

Identify each interval.

- Circle 2 for the 2nd.
- Circle 3 for the 3rd.
- Circle 4 for the 4th.

1

2   3   (4)

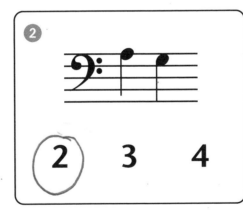

2

(2)   3   4

3

2   (3)   4

Staccato

Use with page 12.

Your teacher will play three melodies.

- Add a dot below each treble clef note that is played staccato.
- Add a dot above each bass clef note that is played staccato.

NOTE TO TEACHER: Play all quarter notes staccato.

Slurs

Using a **red** crayon, color the hand that plays the example.

Using a **black** crayon, trace the slur.

Then play the example on the keyboard.

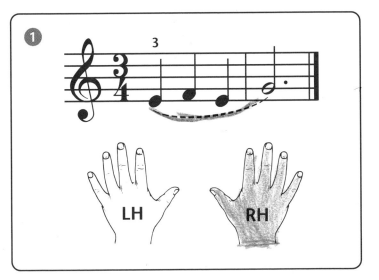

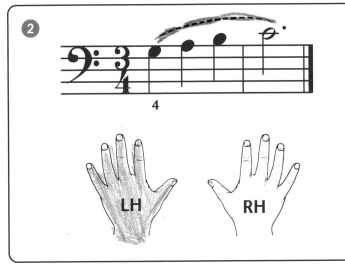

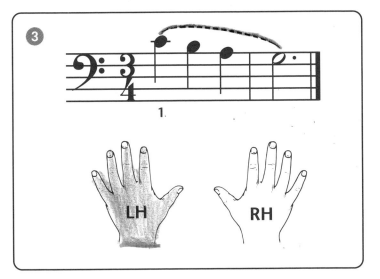

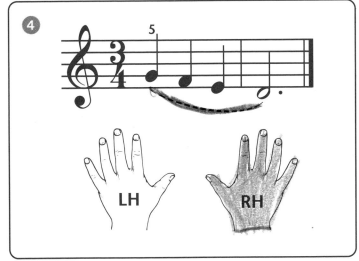

Treble G with Fingers 1 and 5

Use with page 14.

Using an **orange** crayon, color each hat containing a G that is played with finger 1.

Using a **yellow** crayon, color each hat containing a G that is played with finger 5.

Staccato and Legato

Your teacher will play five notes.

- Circle Nannerl Mouse if the notes are played STACCATO.
- Circle Clara Schumann-Cat if the notes are played LEGATO.

1

2

3

4

NOTE TO TEACHER: Play the five notes from the RH or LH C Position, Middle C Position or G Position either staccato or legato.

Treble Clef G, A and B

1. Color the Treble Clef G on the keyboard and staff **orange**.

2. Color the Treble Clef A on the keyboard and staff **blue**.

3. Color the Treble Clef B on the keyboard and staff **purple**.

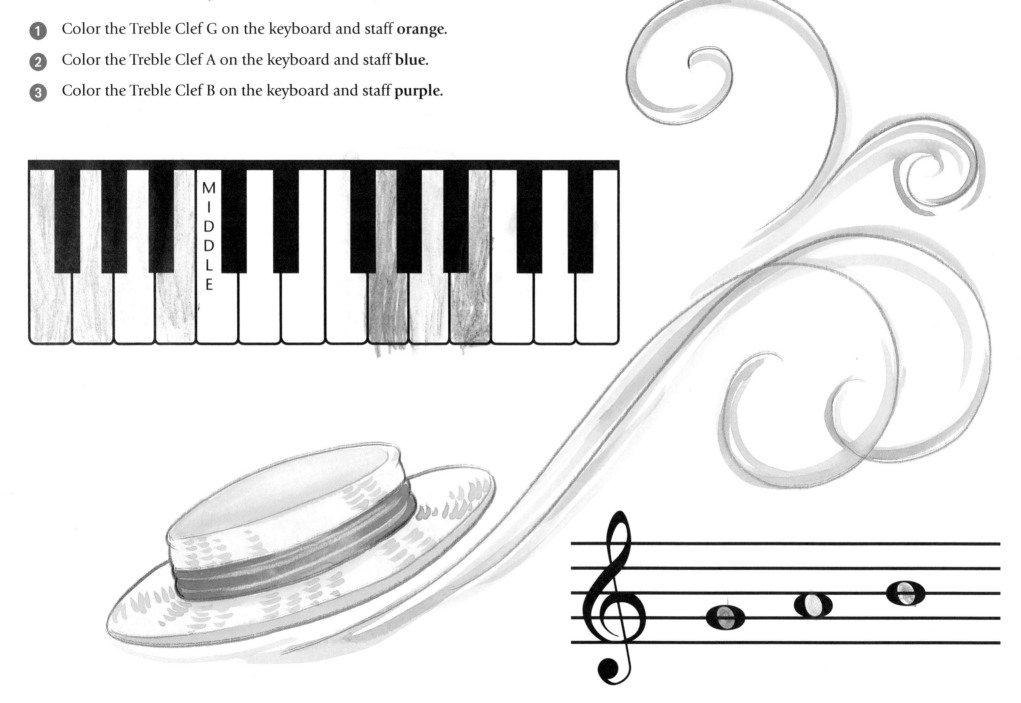

Low G

① Color TREBLE CLEF G **red.**

② Color BASS CLEF G **yellow.**

③ Color LOW G **blue.**

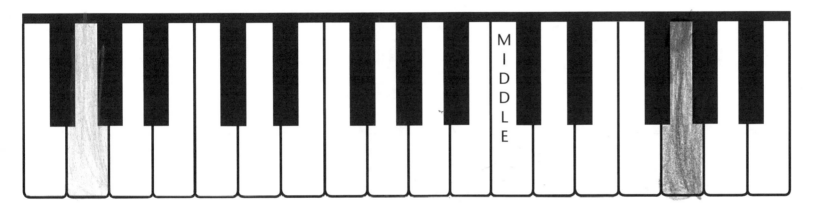

Staccato and Legato Melodies

Use with page 18.

Your teacher will play STACCATO or LEGATO melodies.

● Circle the melody that you hear.

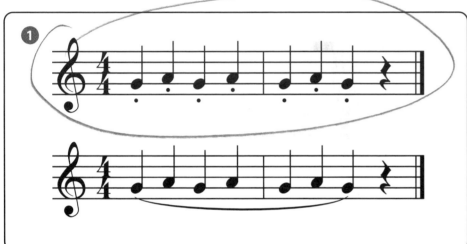

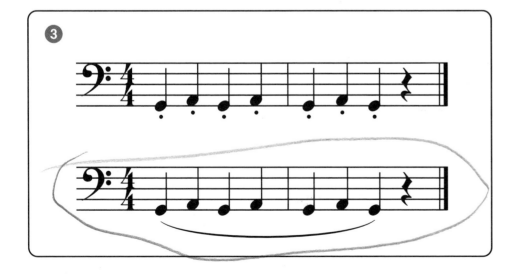

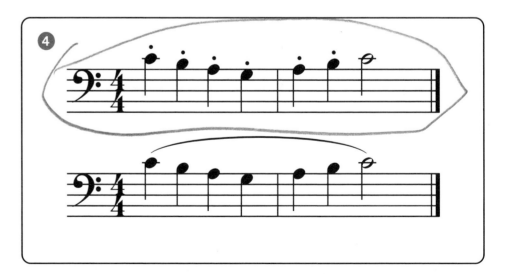

Low G, A and B

① Color the Low G on the keyboard and staff **orange**.

② Color the Low A on the keyboard and staff **blue**.

③ Color the Low B on the keyboard and staff **purple**.

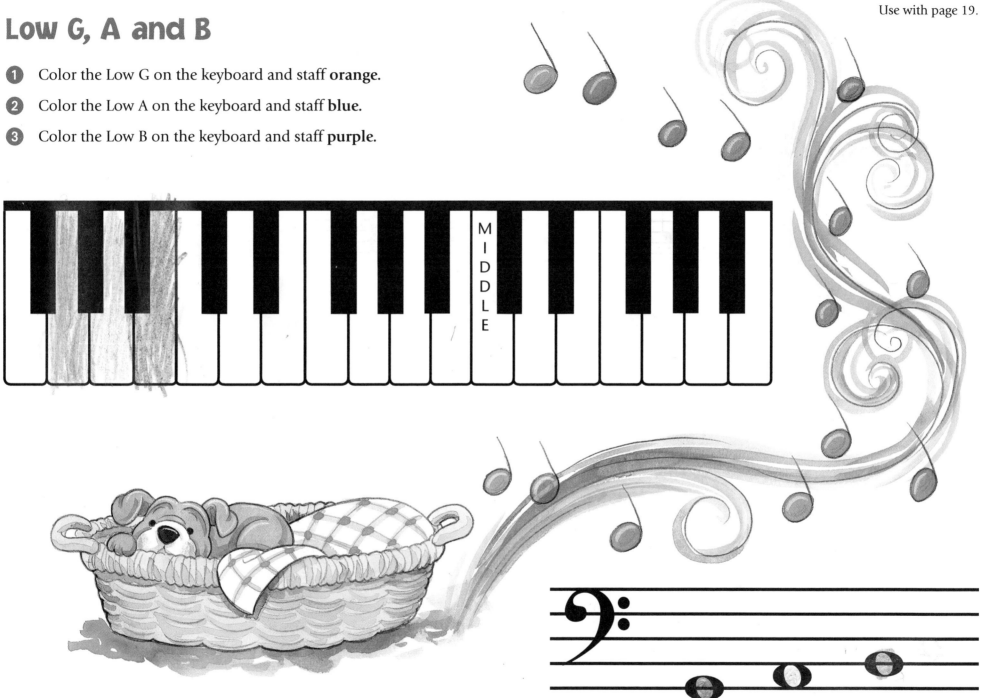

Middle C and Treble Clef C

1 Color the areas containing MIDDLE C **yellow**.

2 Color the areas containing TREBLE CLEF C **orange**.

Treble Clef D

1 Color TREBLE CLEF D **yellow.**

2 Color MIDDLE D **pink.**

3 Color BASS CLEF D **brown.**

G Position for the Right Hand

Use with page 22.

Using a **red** crayon, color G, A, B, C and D from the Right Hand G Position.

G Position for the Right Hand

1. Color the areas containing a G **green**.
2. Color the areas containing an A **red**.
3. Color the areas containing a B **gray**.
4. Color the areas containing a C **black**.
5. Color the areas containing a D **blue**.

Use with page 24.

Harmonic Intervals

Draw lines connecting the dots on the matching boxes.

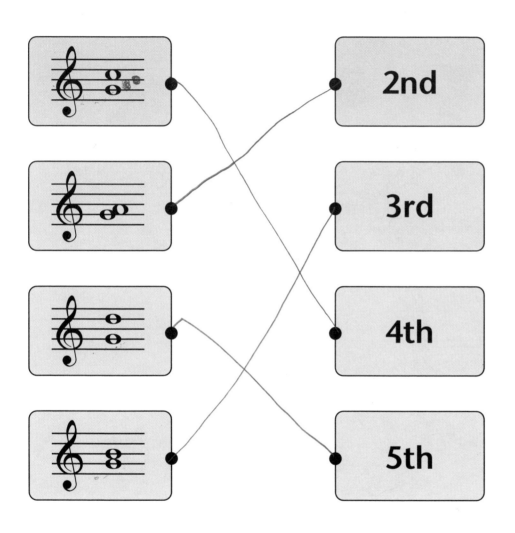

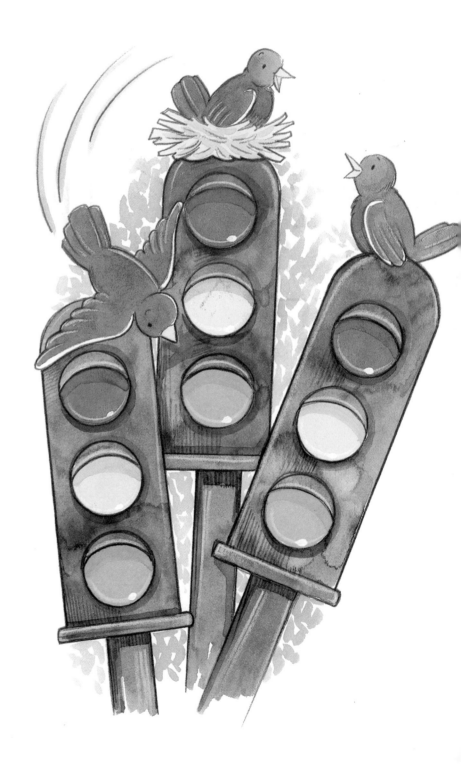

G Position for the Left Hand

Using a **blue** crayon, color G, A, B, C and D from the Left Hand G Position.

G Position for the Left Hand

Use with page 26.

❶ Color the areas containing a G **blue**.

❷ Color the areas containing an A **pink**.

❸ Color the areas containing a B **green**.

❹ Color the areas containing a C **yellow**.

❺ Color the areas containing a D **purple**.

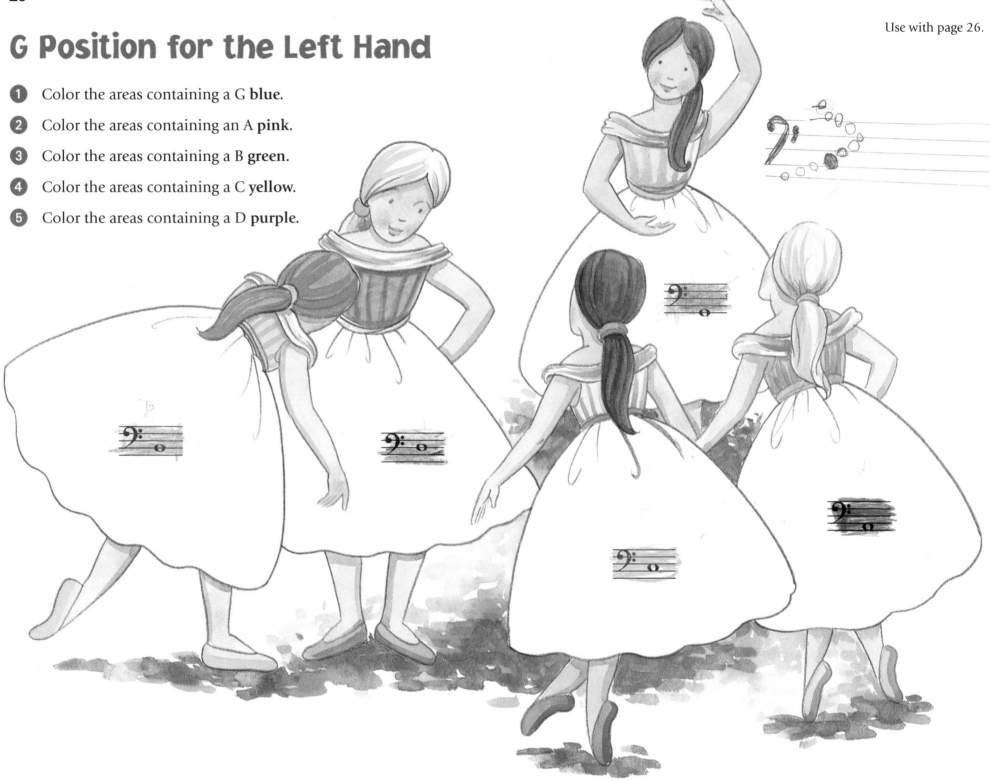

Use with page 27.

Melodic Intervals

Draw lines connecting the dots on the matching boxes.

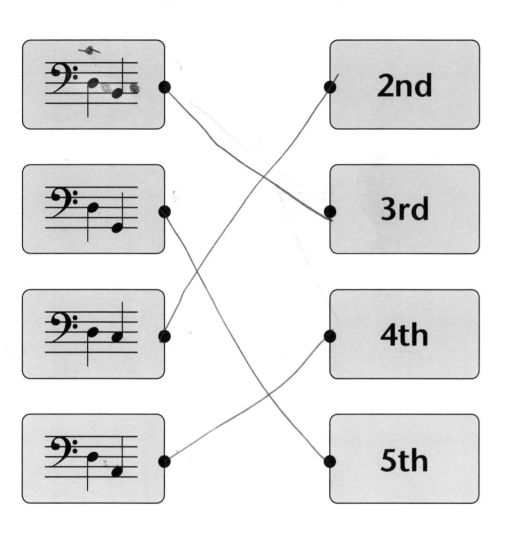

2nd

3rd

4th

5th

G Position

Use with page 28.

Draw lines connecting the dots on the matching boxes.

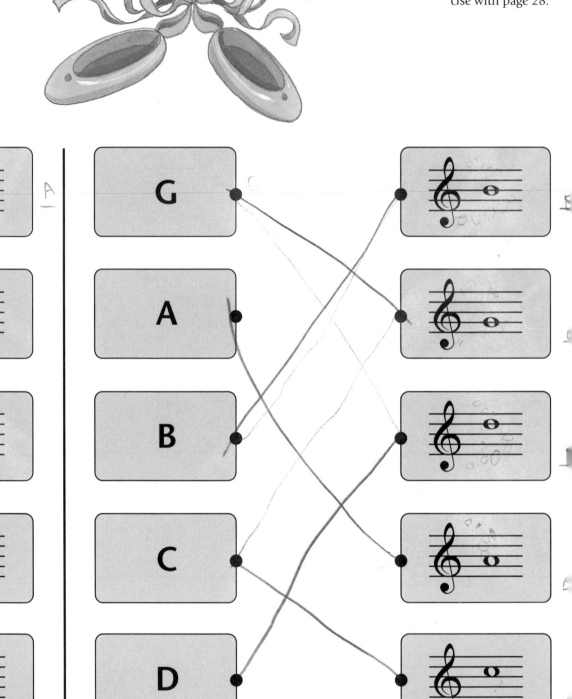

Same and Different

Circle Beethoven Bear if the intervals are the same.

Circle Mozart Mouse if the intervals are different.

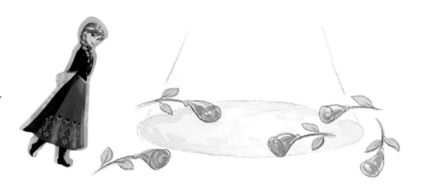

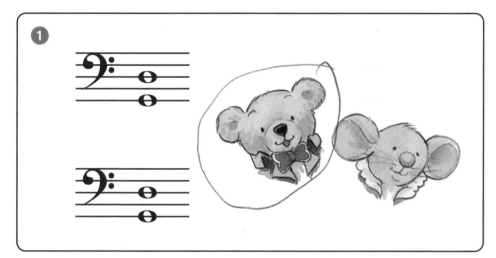

Use with page 30.

Flat Sign

Using a **black** crayon, trace each flat.

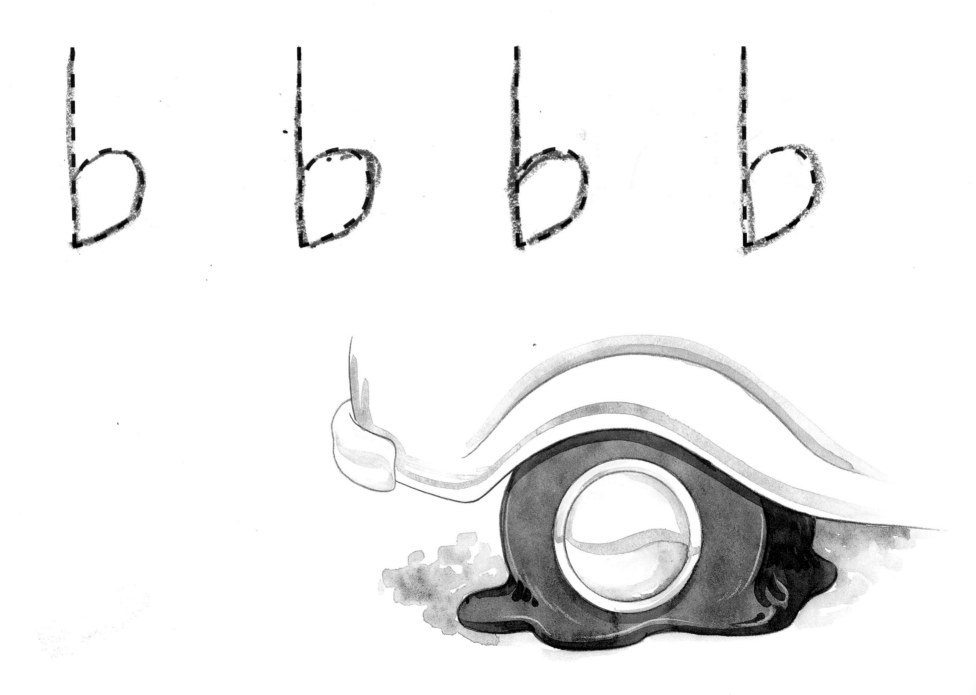

Flats on the Keyboard

1 Color each B-flat **purple**.

2 Color each E-flat **red**.

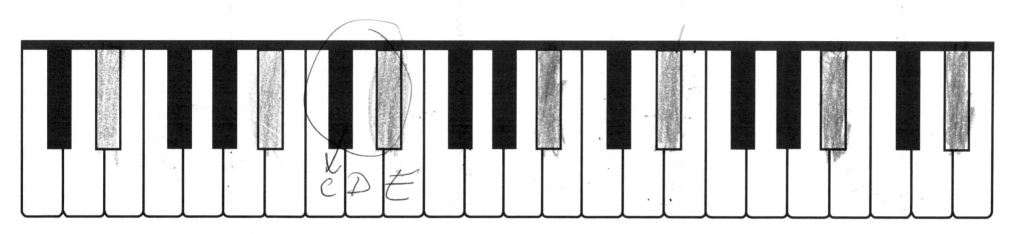

Use with page 32.

Flats on the Grand Staff

1 Circle each B-flat with a **purple** crayon.

2 Circle each E-flat with a **red** crayon.

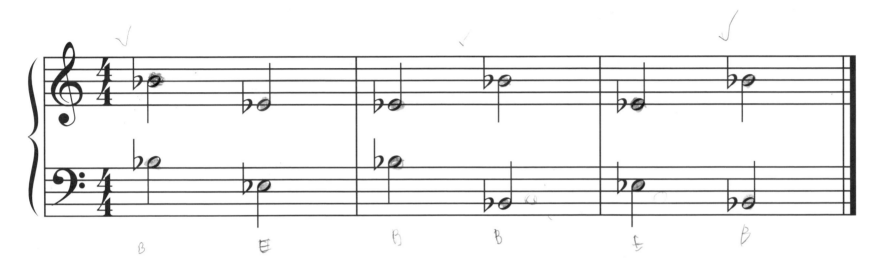

Sharp Sign

Using a **black** crayon, trace each sharp.

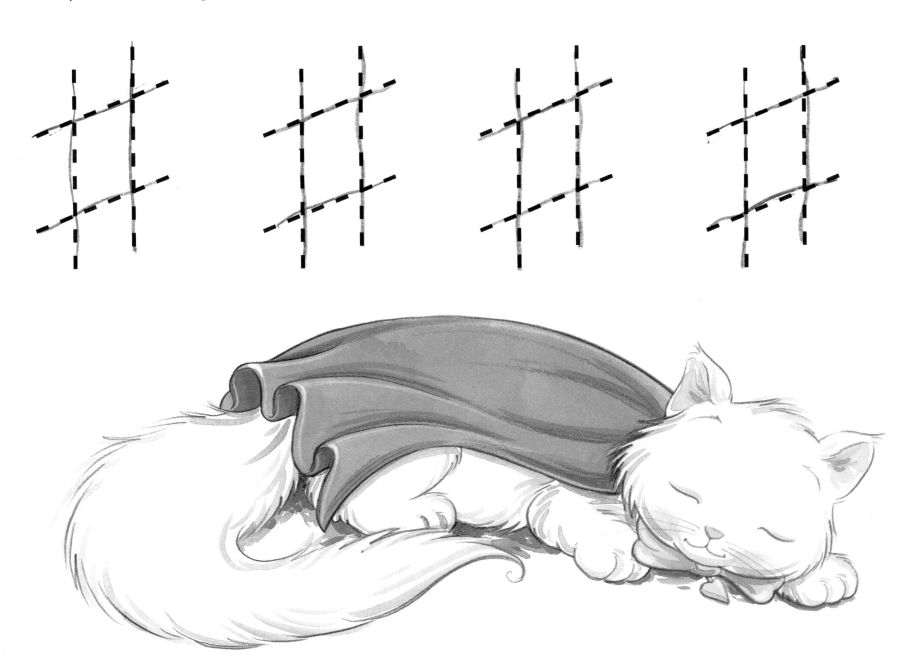

Use with page 34.

Sharps on the Keyboard

1 Color each F-sharp **pink**.

2 Color each D-sharp **yellow**.

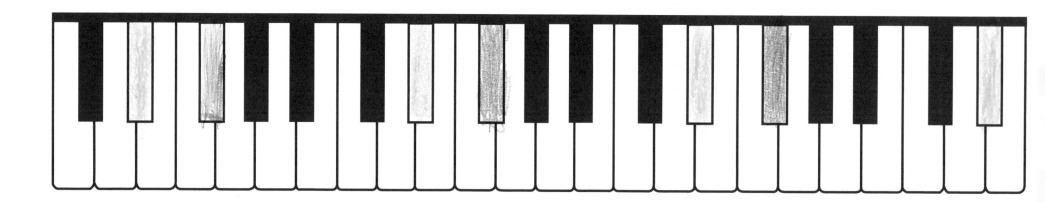

Sharps on the Grand Staff

1 Circle each F-sharp with a **pink** crayon.

2 Circle each D-sharp with an **yellow** crayon.

3 Circle each C-sharp with a **green** crayon.

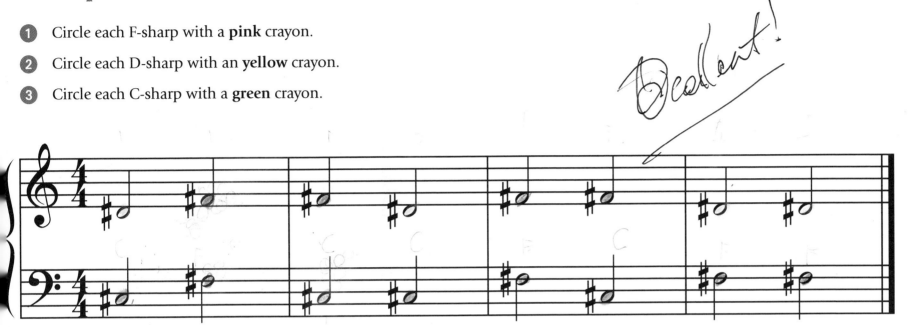

Sharp Sign, Flat Sign, and Tied Notes

1 Color the areas containing a sharp sign **red**.

2 Color the areas containing a flat sign **black**.

3 Color the areas containing tied notes **blue**.

Use with page 37.

Tied Notes

1 Using a **black** crayon, trace the curved line to make tied notes.

2 Using a **red** crayon, circle the letter name of the tied notes.

D E F

D E **F**

38

Rhythm Patterns

Your teacher will clap a rhythm pattern.

- Circle the pattern that you hear.

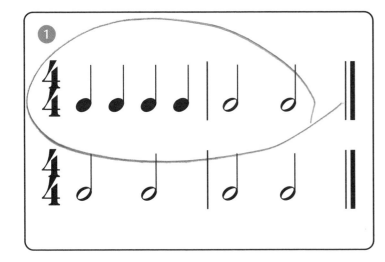

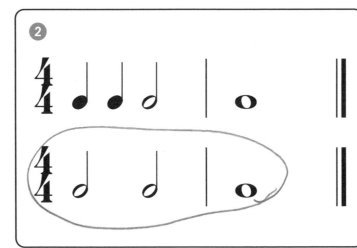

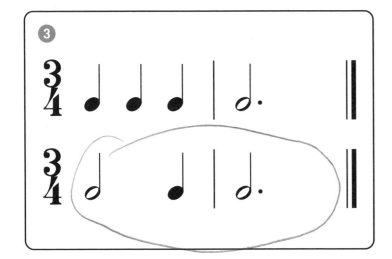

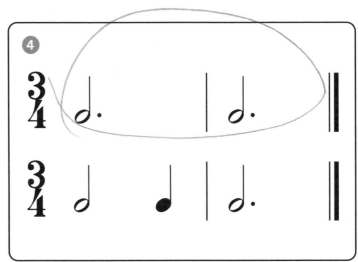

Crescendo

1 Using a **black** crayon, trace the crescendo (———) sign.

2 Using a **red** crayon, trace the mezzo forte (***mf***) sign.

3 Using a **blue** crayon, trace the forte (***f***) sign.

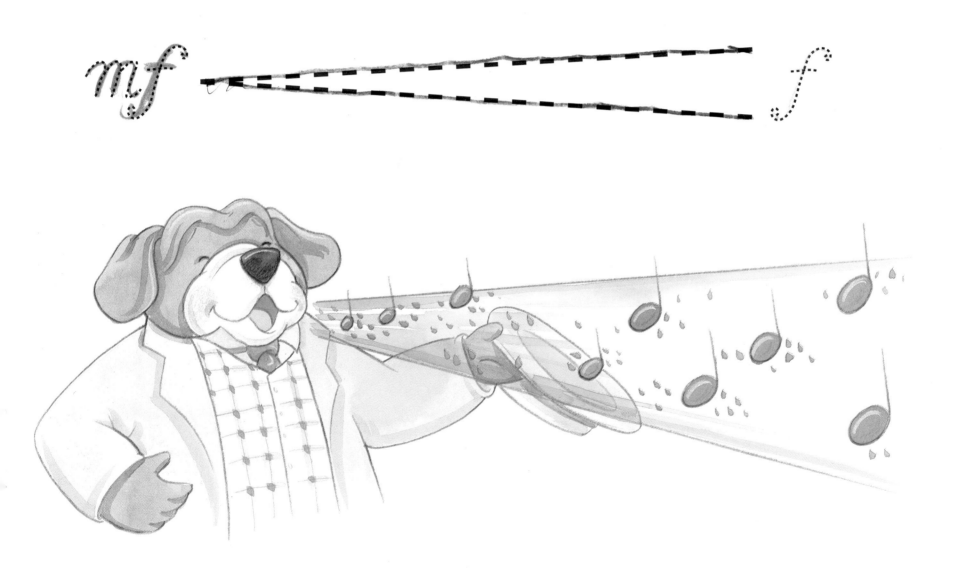

3rds, 4ths and 5ths

Use with page 40.

Draw lines connecting the dots on the matching boxes.

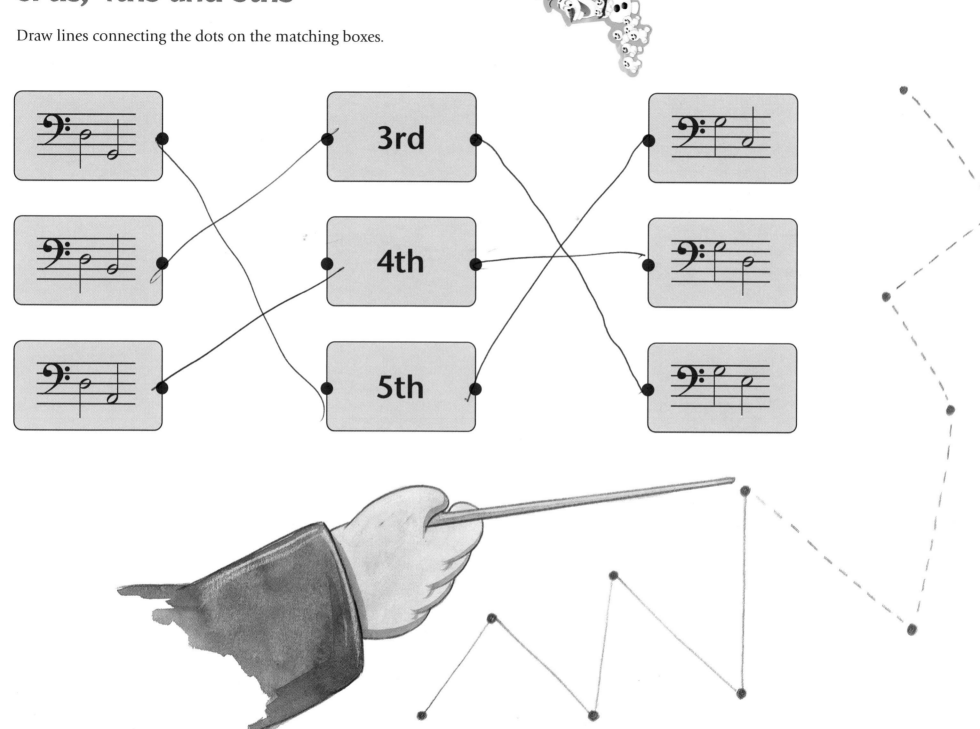

Diminuendo

1 Using a **black** crayon, trace the diminuendo (▷) sign.

2 Using an **orange** crayon, trace the forte (*f*) sign.

3 Using a **purple** crayon, trace the mezzo forte (*mf*) sign.

Melodies with 2nds, 3rds, 4ths and 5ths

Use with page 42.

Your teacher will play melodies with 2nds, 3rds, 4ths and 5ths.

● Circle the melody that you hear.

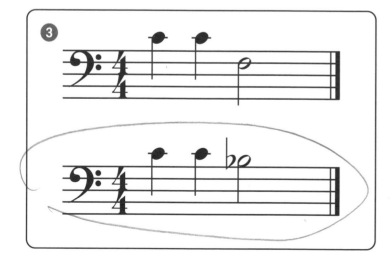

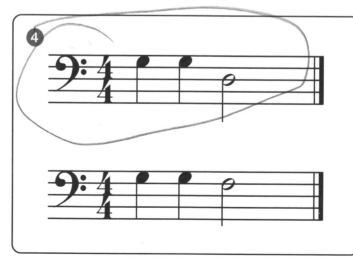

G Position

1 Color the areas containing a G **orange.**

2 Color the areas containing an A **pink.**

3 Color the areas containing a B **green.**

4 Color the areas containing a C **blue.**

5 Color the areas containing a D **yellow.**

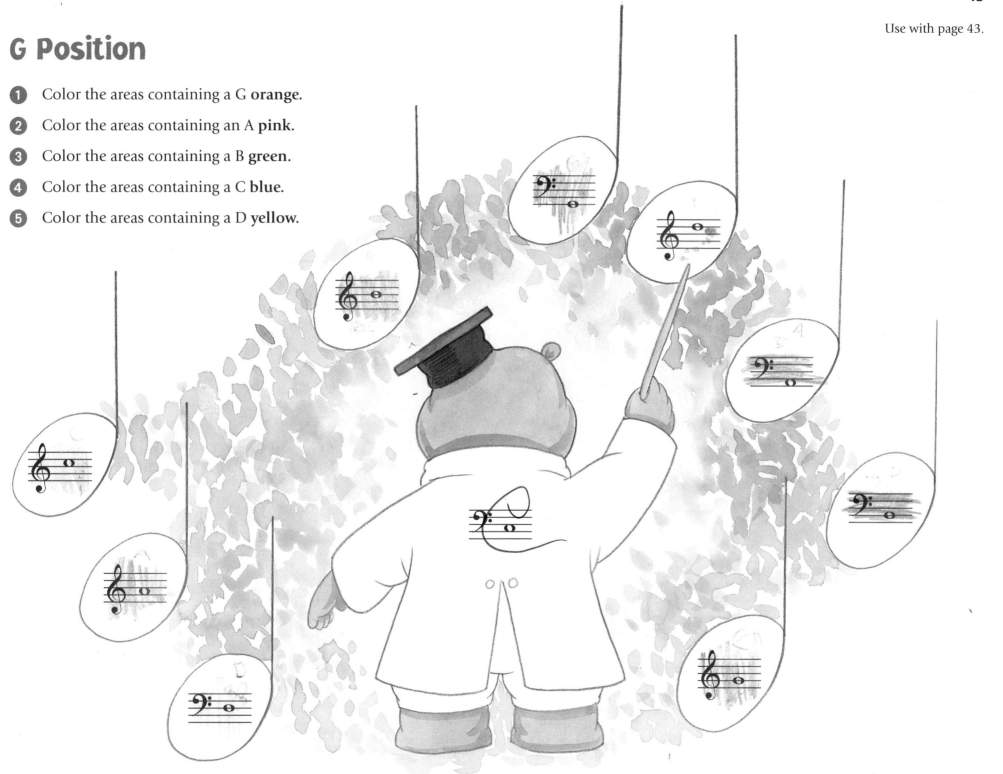

44

Use with page 44.

Tied Notes and Slurs

1 Using a **black** crayon, trace each curved line.

2 Circle **T** for tied notes or **S** for slurs.

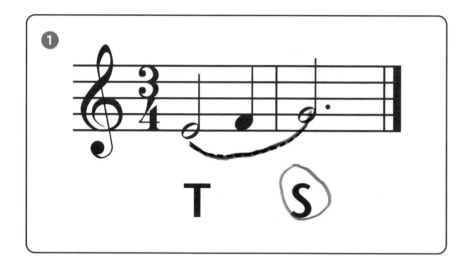

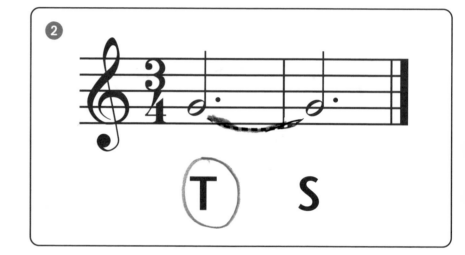

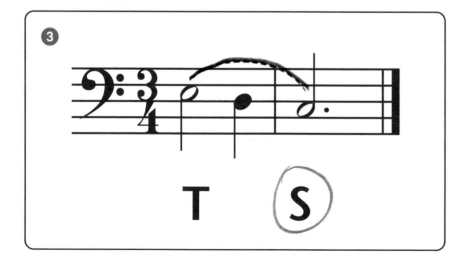

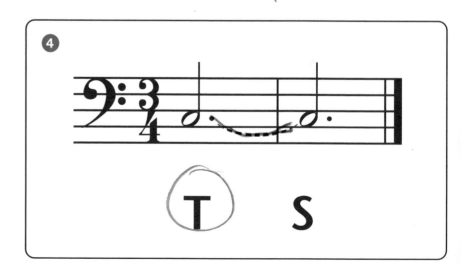

Crescendo and Diminuendo

Your teacher will play four melodies.

- Circle the crescendo sign if the melody gets gradually louder.

- Circle the diminuendo sign if the melody gets gradually softer.

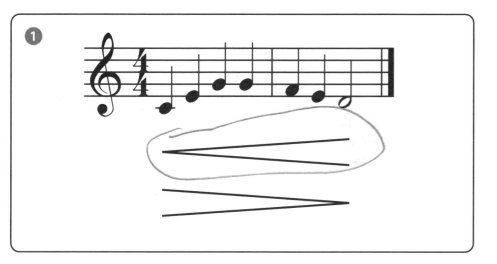

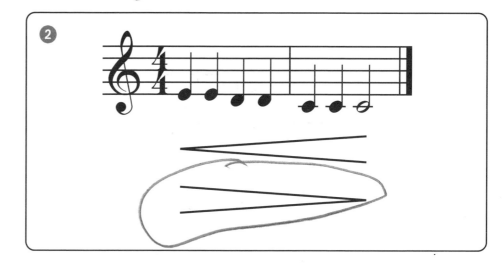

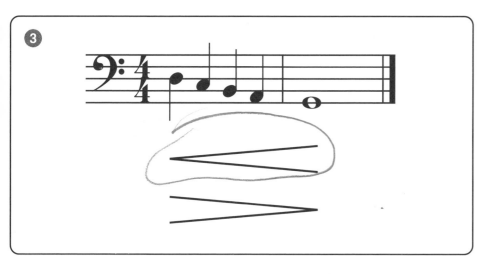

Staccato and Legato

Use with pages 46–47.

Using a **brown** crayon, circle each staccato melody.

Using a **gray** crayon, circle each legato melody.

Then play the example on the keyboard.

1

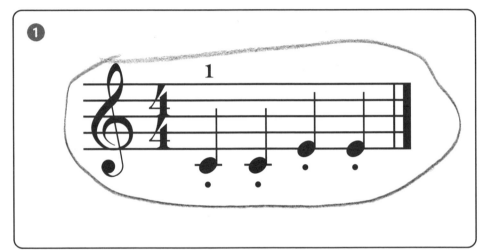

2

3

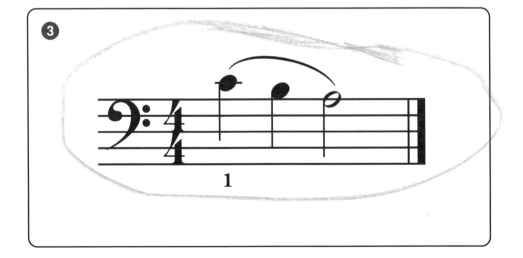

4

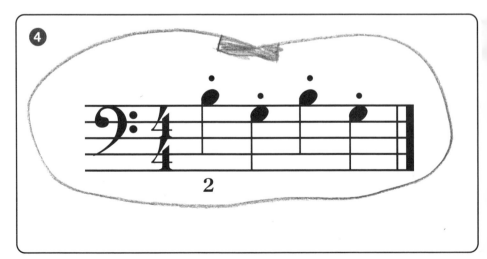

Use with pages 46–47.

Rhythm Patterns

Your teacher will clap a rhythm pattern.

● Circle the pattern that you hear.

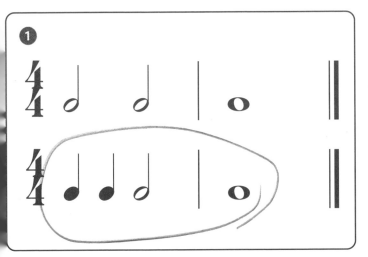

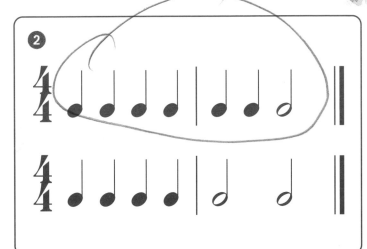

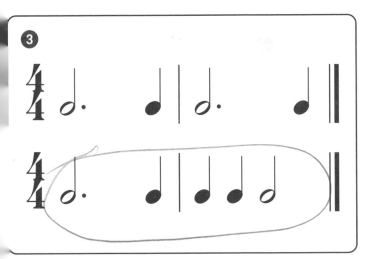

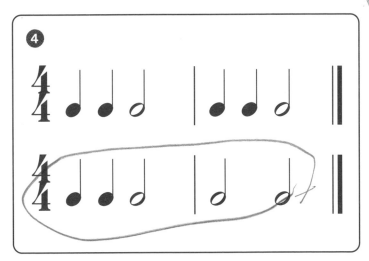

C Position, G Position and Middle C Position

1. Color the areas containing an A **red**.

2. Color the areas containing a B **gray**.

3. Color the areas containing a C **green**.

4. Color the areas containing a D **blue**.

5. Color the areas containing an E **brown**.

6. Color the areas containing an F **yellow**.

7. Color the areas containing a G **orange**.

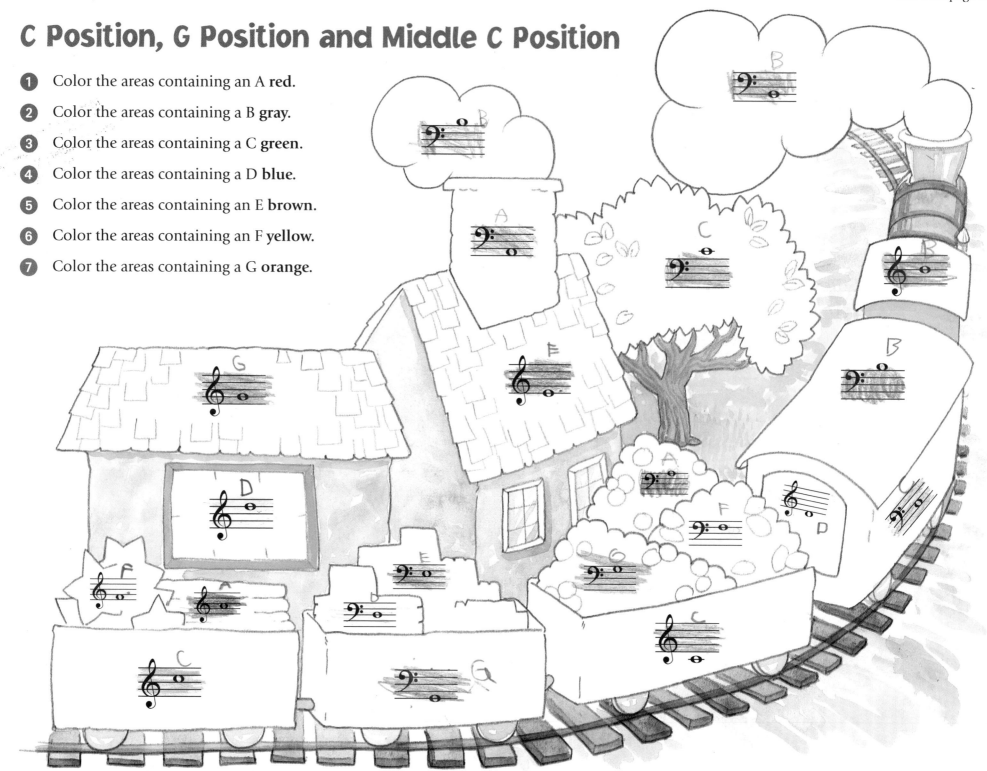